RESEARCH BALLOONS

RESEARCH BALLOONS

Exploring Hidden Worlds

Carole S. Briggs

Lerner Publications Company • Minneapolis

Library of Congress Cataloging-in-Publication Data

Briggs, Carole S.
    Research balloons : exploring hidden worlds /
    Carole S. Briggs.
        p.   cm.
    Includes index.
    Summary: Describes different kinds of research balloons
and the remarkable work that they do in expanding our
knowledge of the world.
    ISBN 0-8225-1585-7 (lib. bdg.)
    1. Balloons, Sounding—Juvenile literature. 2. Balloons in
astronomy—Juvenile literature. [1. Balloons, Sounding.
2. Balloons in astronomy.] I. Title.
TL631.B75 1988   87-17357
551.5'028—dc19   CIP
                                        AC
Manufactured in the United States of America

    2   3   4   5   6   7   8   9   10   97   96   95   94   93   92   91   90   89

Contents

Carrying the first to fly—a sheep, a duck, and a rooster—the Montgolfiers' balloon rises above the crowd at Versailles on September 19, 1783.

1

Inventing the Balloon

For centuries, humans have been fascinated with the idea of flying. Some people designed wings to be attached to a person's arms. Others watched smoke rise from fires and thought there must be a way for them to rise with it. These people tried to build balloons.

Finally, in 1783, two brothers in France successfully built and launched a balloon. Joseph Montgolfier and his younger brother, Jacques-Etienne, were paper makers in Annonay, France. They often talked about constructing a large, paper globe that would float passengers above the earth. The Montgolfiers thought that smoke was a kind of lighter-than-air gas, so they decided to raise their balloon with smoke from burning rags. Actually, smoke rises because air warmed by fire is lighter than the surrounding cooler air. Therefore, a balloon full of hot air will rise until thinner air at higher altitudes can no longer push up on the balloon or until the balloon's hot air cools enough to make it too heavy to stay aloft.

Although people in earlier centuries tried to construct balloons—and the Incas or Chinese may have succeeded in launching them—the Montgolfiers are credited with inventing the balloon. They received a good deal of public attention because both they and their rival, Jacques Charles, wanted to be the first to send up a balloon. The Montgolfiers won the race to fly on June 5, 1783, and their balloon's flight —without passengers—was officially witnessed and documented by the Academy of Sciences.

On September 19, 1783, the Montgolfiers flew their invention—later called a *montgolfier* or a hot-air balloon—before King Louis XVI and his court in Versailles. On this second flight, the balloon carried three passengers— a sheep, a duck, and a rooster. The balloon measured 41 feet (12 meters) in diameter and was 86 feet (26 m) high. Floating to a height of 1,450 feet (435 m), the balloon stayed in the air for about 10 minutes. After the balloon's

Joseph Montgolfier

Jacques-Etienne Montgolfier

air cooled, it descended slowly, and the animal passengers landed safely. During both flights, the balloons were *tethered* or tied to the ground with a long cord.

Jacques Charles was not discouraged by the Montgolfiers' success. He continued with his own plans to launch a balloon, but he was not going to use smoke to get his balloon aloft. He had another idea.

Seventeen years earlier, the English scientist Henry Cavendish had discovered a new gas by dropping acid on iron scraps. He filled one animal bladder with air from the atmosphere and another with this new gas. Then he weighed the bladders. The new gas was 11 times lighter! Cavendish named

his discovery inflammable air; today it is called hydrogen.

Jacques Charles decided to power his balloon with the new inflammable air. His redesigned *gasbag*, or envelope, was made from silk and lined with an elastic gum, and it was closed at the bottom to keep the gas from escaping.

As a balloon rises higher, the air is thinner, so the gas expands. The air is also colder at higher altitudes, which eventually makes the gas contract, and the balloon descends. These two opposing forces allowed Charles to control his balloon.

Charles' balloon was launched on August 27, 1783. It was the first balloon inflated with hydrogen rather than hot air. Unlike the Montgolfiers'

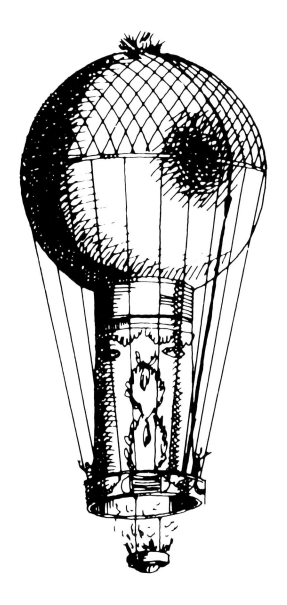

A drawing of an early hot-air balloon. Passengers stand in the gondola that surrounds the fire in the central grate.

balloons, Charles' balloon was not tethered. It ascended 3,000 feet (900 m) and flew a distance of 15 miles (24 kilometers). Although Charles was not the first to successfully launch a balloon, he and his partners, Jean and Noel Robert, are credited with the invention of the gas balloon.

The first person to ride in a balloon was another Frenchman, Pilatre de Rozier. In the hot-air balloon designed by the Montgolfiers, de Rozier rose to a height of 80 feet (24 m) on October 15, 1783, and stayed aloft for five minutes. De Rozier stood at the side of the *gondola*, or passenger compartment, and a fire in a central grate provided the hot air. His tethered flight was recorded by the Academy of Sciences. On November 21, 1783, de Rozier and the Marquis d'Arlandes made the first untethered flight across Paris and the surrounding countryside. Then, on December 1, 1783, Jacques Charles made the first free flight in a gas balloon. He flew over Paris and, two hours later, landed in the country town of Nesle, 27 miles (43 km) away.

It was not long before "balloon fever" spread across the Atlantic Ocean to the United States. Prominent Americans such as Benjamin Franklin and Thomas Jefferson were in France at the time, and they wrote letters home giving enthusiastic reports of the flights they had witnessed. When he returned to the United States, Dr. John Foulke, an American who had studied medicine in France, decided to build his own hot-air balloon. On May 10, 1784, he

The first humans to fly, the Marquis d'Arlandes and Pilatre de Rozier, wave to the crowds at the Bois de Boulogne near Paris. Thirty minutes after taking off, the montgolfier landed in a field.

sent his first free-floating balloon aloft over Philadelphia.

Like the race in France between Charles and the Montgolfiers, a contest to send up a piloted balloon began in the United States. Dr. Foulke and some of his colleagues decided to make a silk balloon that could carry people. A lawyer named Peter Carnes decided to do the same.

On June 24, 1784, in Baltimore, Maryland, Carnes flew his balloon several times in front of a large crowd. His flights, however, were unpiloted and tethered. The onlookers shouted for Carnes to get into the gondola, but Carnes weighed 234 pounds (105 kilograms), and he had already discovered in several earlier private attempts that the balloon would not go very high with him on board. As the crowd became more demanding, a 13-year-old boy named Edward Warren volunteered to go up in the tethered balloon and thus became the first person to fly over American soil.

These early balloon flights in France and the United States proved that it was indeed possible for human beings to fly. Now people began to wonder if balloon flights could have any practical uses.

Peter Carnes launches the first balloon to fly in North America. Carnes later launched his balloon with its first passenger, Edward Warren.

An advertisement for a balloon flight in the 1800s. This poster announces an evening ascent by Margaret Graham from the Royal Gardens, a London amusement park.

2

Exploring the Lower Atmosphere

As balloon flights became more common, they were most often used for entertainment. Both women and men became *aeronauts*, or balloon pilots, and many of them treated ballooning as a circus performance. They advertised their flights and sold tickets to onlookers, amazing audiences with their ability to fly.

Some aeronauts, however, wanted to learn more about the earth's atmosphere. If one flew higher, how much would the temperature of the air change? How did the direction and speed of the wind vary? How would air pressure change high up in the atmosphere?

The first record of a balloon being used for scientific investigation was in August 1784 when a French chemist, Guyton de Moreau, and his partner, Abbe Bertrand, ascended to over 10,000 feet (3,000 m) to collect data on atmospheric temperature and pressure. Using a thermometer and *barograph*, an instrument that measures variations of air pressure in relation to altitude,

they observed that both air pressure and temperature decreased as they went higher.

In 1804, Joseph Louis Gay-Lussac made two balloon trips from Paris to study the makeup of the atmosphere and the earth's magnetism. On one flight, soaring to 23,000 feet (6,900 m), Gay-Lussac felt his heartbeat grow more rapid as he rose higher. He had trouble breathing and he fainted. Then his balloon drifted back to earth as the surrounding upper air cooled the hydrogen.

For the next 50 years, no one dared go higher than 23,000 feet (6,900 m). During that time, changes were made in balloon design, which gave gas balloon pilots more control over how high they would go and when they would land. To control ascent, balloons carried *ballast*. Ballast could be anything heavy, often sand. A pilot simply threw sandbags out of the gondola to make the balloon lighter. This caused it to rise. To control descent, a small valve was installed at the top of a balloon. Pilots would pull a cord that opened the valve to let gas escape. This made the balloon less buoyant, and it would slowly descend. *Valving* is still used in all piloted balloons and in some radio-controlled balloons as well.

Finally, in 1862, aeronaut Henry Coxwell and scientist James Glaisher could not resist attempting an altitude record. While flying their gas balloon to nearly 30,000 feet (9,000 m) above the English Midlands, Glaisher fainted

James Glaisher and Henry Coxwell's first balloon flight.

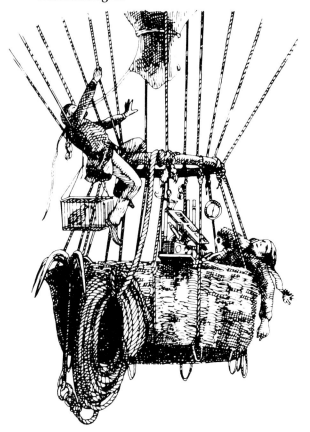

from lack of oxygen. Coxwell, however, managed to pull the valve line with his teeth and release enough hydrogen to bring the balloon down.

Undaunted, Coxwell and Glaisher made 26 more flights to learn about the lower atmosphere. On some flights, they used a *hygrometer* to measure the amount of water vapor at different altitudes. On others, they used a thermometer to measure air temperature at different altitudes. They learned that the colder the air, the less moisture it holds, and that when the air is full of as much moisture as it can hold, clouds form. They discovered that clouds usually form at 1,000 to 50,000 feet (300-15,000 m) where air is colder than at sea level. Coxwell and Glaisher also classified clouds according to their appearance and height.

In 1875, scientists Theodore Sivel and Joseph Croce-Spinelli attempted to better Glaisher and Coxwell's high-altitude record. Ascending from Paris, France, they used oxygen-filled bladders with mouthpieces for breathing but, unfortunately, did not carry enough oxygen. When their balloon, the *Zenith*, rose to 28,000 feet (8,400 m), Sivel, Croce-Spinelli, and aeronaut Gaston Tissandier, all fainted. As the balloon descended into a more oxygen-rich atmosphere, Tissandier woke up and discovered that his two companions were dead.

This tragedy all but stopped high-altitude ballooning, but it did not diminish scientific curiosity. Continuing as leaders in developing technology,

Sivel (left) cuts the ballast loose while Tissandier (center) observes the barometers and Croce-Spinelli takes a breath of oxygen.

the French began using large, mechanized, *meteorological balloons* to study the atmosphere in 1892.

Meteorological balloons carried instruments to record temperature and altitude. These balloons often rose to an altitude of 8 to 10 miles (13-16 km). Because there was little air pressure on the balloon's surface at that height, the hydrogen would expand to fill the gasbag. Then the gas automatically would begin to *vent*, or escape, out the bottom of the bag. Because the hydrogen leaked out so slowly, balloons often drifted up to 700 miles (1,120 km) away from their launch sites before landing. Therefore, recovering the recording instruments was not always easy.

To solve this problem, German aeronaut-meteorologist William F. Assmann designed *expandable balloons* made of rubber. Closed at the bottom, each balloon carried instruments sealed in a wicker box suspended in a hoop. When the gas expanded beyond the gasbag's capacity, the balloon would burst and a parachute would open and float the instruments back to earth. Parachutes descend more quickly than balloons, so the instruments from an expandable balloon would land closer to the launch site.

Blue Hill Observatory

In 1885, Abbot Lawrence Rotch founded the Blue Hill Observatory. Located about 10 miles (16 km) south of Boston, Massachusetts, on the top of the Great Blue Hill, the observatory would use kites and meteorological balloons to provide weather information. The observatory consisted of a round brick tower attached to a low, square building that looked like an old castle.

At first, Rotch and his three colleagues —Henry Helm Clayton, Sterling P. Fergusson, and Willard P. Gerrish— observed cloud appearances and heights and the weather that accompanied

15

each kind of cloud formation from the ground. Then, in 1894, they sent aloft a kite that carried a *thermograph*, a device designed to record air temperature at different altitudes. These scientists launched more than 80 box kites during 1896 and, in 1900, they sent a kite to a record altitude of 16,050 feet (4,815 m).

Aware that the French were using gas balloons for atmospheric studies, Rotch longed to do the same. Balloons launched from Blue Hill Observatory, however, could easily drift over the Atlantic Ocean, losing their cargo, or *payloads*, in the sea. Rotch decided to launch his balloon from a safer location and sent his colleague, Sterling P. Fergusson, to the Louisiana Purchase Exposition in St. Louis, Missouri. Fergusson launched the first U.S. weather balloon on September 15, 1905. The expandable balloon burst at an altitude of 56,815 feet (17,045 m), and its payload landed 50 miles (80 km) from the launch site. The instruments had recorded temperature, air pressure, and altitude and showed that air temperature stops falling at an altitude of 8 to 10 miles (13-16 km) above sea level.

Between 1905 and 1908, over 80 balloon flights supervised by the Blue Hill Observatory team were launched from St. Louis and later from Pittsfield, Massachusetts, a city farther inland than Boston. Most flights lasted from two to three hours, and the balloons usually rose 8 to 10 miles (13-16 km). Very few balloons were lost, and few instruments were damaged.

After Rotch's death in 1912, the observatory was donated to Harvard University. Routine measurements, or *soundings*, of atmospheric conditions at various heights were made by balloon flights at Blue Hill until the beginning of World War I, when all available money was channeled into the war effort.

Meteorological Balloons

During the 1930s, balloon-borne meteorological instruments were put back in use. Old instruments were improved, and new ones were designed. One new device was the *radiosonde*. As a balloon rose, a radiosonde would send out a series of coded electrical impulses that indicated changes in temperature, air pressure, and relative humidity. The radiosonde in use today is similar, but it also has an automatic tracking antenna, a *theodolite*, which allows meteorologists to compute the altitude of the radiosonde and the upper air wind speed and direction.

Meteorological balloons in use today are made of high-quality neoprene rubber. Like Assmann's expandable balloon, they are closed at the bottom so, when they reach the desired altitude, the ever-expanding gas will fill the gasbag, causing it to burst.

Weather balloons are usually inflated inside special buildings that have been designed to shield balloons from the wind. First, a launch specialist inserts the empty balloon into a fiberglass cylinder, and then a member of

In 1936, the U.S. Navy used this radio-sonde to measure changes in air temperature, pressure, and humidity.

the launch crew turns on the pump switch connected to tanks of helium. Slowly the balloon fills with helium and emerges from the top of the cylinder, as if someone chewing gum were blowing an enormous bubble. When the balloon is properly inflated, it rises enough to pull on the line attached to the pump switch, shutting it off. As it leaves the cylinder, the balloon begins to rise through an opening in the roof. A payload of instruments is attached, and the balloon drifts quickly upward, becoming a tiny dot against the sky.

Most balloons carrying radiosondes measure 5 feet (1.5 m) in diameter at launching. Often they stretch to 20 feet (6 m) before bursting, sending their payloads back to earth by parachute. The exact design of a radiosonde can vary. Some mechanically code data for transmission to the ground, while others produce direct electrical impulses. All types of radiosondes, however, provide valuable information on temperature, pressure, humidity, and wind speeds at various altitudes up to 100,000 feet (30,000 m).

Twice each day, hundreds of balloons carrying radiosondes are launched by meteorological stations throughout the world. This is part of the upper-air program of the World Meteorological Organization. Using the information provided by radiosondes, local meteorologists track world weather patterns and make accurate weather forecasts. Unlike satellites, balloons can record readings at several different altitudes during a flight.

The safesonde, a portable radio balloon system, measures air temperature, humidity, and wind speed. The balloon is launched from a cylinder (upper left) and slowly emerges (lower left and lower right) until it is properly inflated. Then it rises into the air (upper right) with its payload of instruments.

Recently, researchers at the University of Wisconsin in Madison have developed a method of measuring wind speed that uses radar to detect the speed of water particles caught in the wind. This "wind-profiler" resembles a half-sized football field full of TV antennas and should eventually give more accurate and current readings of upper-air wind speed than weather balloons. But until it is developed to the point where it can be used on a large scale, weather balloons will continue to be used.

Pollution Drift

Today, low-altitude balloons are also being used to study *pollution drift*. Pollution drift occurs when a cloud of pollution is trapped over a city by a *thermal inversion*—a layer of cool air trapped beneath a layer of warm air—and winds blow the cloud across the countryside.

To follow a cloud of pollution, a balloon needs to remain aloft for more than a few hours, so often a *zero-pressure balloon* is used. Shaped like a teardrop, a zero-pressure balloon is filled with a large bubble of helium gas and is open at the bottom. Ballast is dropped from the balloon to make it go higher. When the helium expands to fill the gasbag, a little of the gas vents out the bottom of the bag, which keeps the balloon at a steady altitude. When there is no longer enough helium to keep the balloon aloft, and the ballast is almost gone, the balloon must

Zero-pressure research balloons are used to conduct a variety of scientific experiments such as measuring pollution and studying cosmic rays.

land. Zero-pressure balloons can be brought down by venting more and more helium. This is done either by the pilot or with the help of radio-controlled instruments.

One pollution drift study was done by artist-aeronaut Vera Simons, along with Dr. Rudolf J. Engelman, chief scientist of the National Oceanic and Atmospheric Administration, and pilot Jimmie Craig. They rose into the polluted sky over St. Louis, Missouri, on June 8, 1976, at 8:55 A.M. Aboard the two-level gondola, Vera Simons and her crew had 4,000 pounds (1,800 kg) of instruments that enabled them to study the elements of the polluted air and where it was drifting.

As the huge silver balloon with its bubble of helium traveled over St. Louis, instruments began sucking air into canisters and bags to analyze the composition of the cloud of pollution. The crew learned that the air around their open gondola contained carbon monoxide, hydrocarbons, and oxides of nitrogen from automobile and industrial exhaust. The air also included sulfur from the city's many smokestacks.

At sunset, the balloonists were still over St. Louis. They were in a thermal inversion, where winds are light, and the immense cloud of pollution motionless. During the night, however, the wind picked up. The deadly cloud and the balloon began to drift eastward over the food-growing plains of Illinois. Chase vans on the ground followed the balloon as it moved. The cloud of pollution drifted across Illinois, and then began to head south over Griffin, Indiana. It had been 24 hours since the balloonists had left the ground, and their balloon had too little helium to remain aloft. They descended by valving

and landed in a wheat field outside of Griffin. The cloud of pollution kept moving on.

In 1978, Thomas Heinsheimer spent $65,000 to construct another balloon to study pollution. The *America* was the world's first *superpressure balloon* that could carry humans. Completely round, the silver balloon had a gasbag made of Mylar, and on board were pollution-measuring instruments similar to those used in Vera Simons' project. The *America* made several flights over California, Arizona, and Utah to measure air contaminants. Because the balloon could stay aloft for many months, Heinsheimer and his copilot, Peter Neushul, were able to follow one drifting pollution cloud from California to Kansas.

A superpressure balloon is another type of low-altitude balloon used for scientific study. Made of very strong plastic and closed at the bottom, it is partially inflated with helium to a point where the pressure inside the gasbag is slightly higher than the pressure of the surrounding air. The balloon then rises until the helium expands to fill the gasbag and displaces an amount of air equal to the amount of helium. At this point, the balloon reaches its cruising altitude, which is determined by the size of the balloon, with larger balloons rising higher and smaller ones reaching lower altitudes. Since it does not need to lose ballast or vent helium, the superpressure balloon will stay in the air until it is torn or the sudden weight of rain or ice brings it down.

While expandable balloons stay up for only a few hours, and zero-pressure balloons will fly up to 40 hours, a superpressure balloon can remain aloft for about a year.

A slightly different kind of superpressure balloon, the Adjustable Buoyancy Balloon Tracer, has recently been developed by Sandia National Laboratories in Albuquerque, New Mexico, to help in the study of acid rain. Its gasbag has two chambers; one is filled with helium and the other with air. Attached to the balloon and controlled by an on-board computer are a small pump and a valve. While other superpressure balloons must stay at a constant altitude, the Tracer's computer-operated altitude control system keeps the balloon following the airflow by instructing the pump valve to take in air or let it out. Because it is heavier than helium, the air acts as ballast. When air is let out, the balloon can rise as high as 18,000 feet (5,400 m). This feature gives researchers a more complete view of how changes in the atmosphere affect acid rain, regional haze, and other long-term forms of air pollution.

Although ballooning began as an entertaining adventure, it has since proved its usefulness in gathering scientific information. And once balloons were successfully used to explore the lower atmosphere, people wanted to send them into the upper atmosphere.

A Sandia balloon tracer is readied for flight. Capable of following an airflow for 1,000 miles (1,600 km) or more, the tracer helps scientists to understand how winds in the upper atmosphere affect acid rain and other forms of long-range air pollution.

Captain Hawthorne Gray (in helmet) prepares for his third attempt at the world altitude record.

3

Soaring into the Upper Atmosphere

Scientists were delighted with the information that balloon flights provided about the air a few miles above the earth's surface. But now they also wanted to know what conditions were like 10 miles (16 km) or more above the ground. They wanted to study *cosmic rays*—streams of high-energy particles—and solar energy.

In 1914, Charles Greeley Abbot decided to send small, expandable balloons into the upper atmosphere. Abbot, the director of the Smithsonian Astrophysical Observatory, was interested in the effects of solar energy on the earth.

Abbot launched his first balloon in July 1914 in Omaha, Nebraska. The balloon's payload included a thermometer that gave readings as the altitude changed and a *pyrheliometer*, an instrument for measuring the amount of energy given off by the sun. Abbot had expected the air to become colder as the balloon rose until the temperature reached absolute zero (-459.67° Fahrenheit, or -273.15° Celsius). Instead,

he discovered that temperatures fell up to an altitude of 7 miles (11 km). Then they remained constant until 12 miles (19 km), when they began to rise. The atmosphere from 7 miles (11 km) to 30 miles (48 km) above the earth is called the *stratosphere*. At 7 miles (11 km) the average temperature is -110° F (-79° C), and it is -18° F (-28° C) at 30 miles (48 km) above the earth's equator.

Once unpiloted balloons reached the stratosphere, the next step was to send up flights with human pilots. Early in the 20th century, people imagined a trip to the stratosphere as people today think of a trip to Mars. Only the most daring would venture that far.

Captain Hawthorne Gray was the first person to pilot a stratospheric expedition. Gray had been trained to fly balloons, airships, and fixed-wing airplanes in the military. He first attempted to reach the dizzying heights of the stratosphere on March 9, 1927, from Scott Field, just outside of Belleville, Illinois.

Gray was determined to set the world record for altitude. Knowing that temperatures would be extremely cold by the time he reached the stratosphere, Gray lumbered out of the hangar dressed in long underwear, two wool shirts, a sweater, a leather flight suit lined with reindeer fleece, and high-topped leather boots. He also wore a leather helmet, an upper-face cover, a mouth mask, goggles, and mittens. People who saw him said he looked like a large brown bear!

Gray carefully inspected his gas balloon. Other than three oxygen tanks, his most important pieces of equipment were two barographs, which would officially record his altitude level.

At 1:18 P.M., Captain Gray gave the signal to dump enough sand ballast for lift-off. As he rose to 25,000 feet (7,500 m), his supply of oxygen began to cool rapidly, making breathing uncomfortable, and he passed out at 27,000 feet (8,100 m). The balloon eventually set a U.S. altitude record of 28,510 feet (8,553 m) but not the world record Gray was attempting.

By the time his balloon came back down to 17,000 feet (5,100 m), Gray had regained consciousness, and was able to slow his rapidly descending craft by dumping ballast. He landed safely at Ashley, Illinois, only 40 miles (64 km) from his takeoff point.

Undaunted, Gray decided to attempt the world record again two months later on May 4, 1927. The record was then held by French aeronaut Jean Callizo at 40,820 feet (12,246 m), and

Gray knew it would be dangerous to fly higher. Other aeronauts had learned that between 40,000 and 50,000 feet (12,000-15,000 m), the reduced air pressure caused lungs to stop functioning and gases to bubble out of the blood, but Gray went anyway.

Forty-five minutes into his flight, Gray reached 40,000 feet (12,000 m). His sand ballast was gone, so he threw out an empty oxygen bottle, and the balloon rose to 42,240 feet (12,672 m) —and the world record. Then the work of trying to come down began. Gray had very little equipment left to use as ballast to slow his descent. His balloon had vented a lot of hydrogen, so it became heavier as it lost altitude, and fell faster and faster.

Gray threw two more oxygen tanks overboard. Then he threw out the radio batteries. The balloon was now at 8,000 feet (2,400 m), and it was still falling too fast to land safely. Climbing onto the edge of the gondola, Gray parachuted to the ground. To his dismay, his altitude record was not considered an official one because he failed to land with his balloon.

Gray made a third try for the record on November 4, 1927. He made a slower ascent this time in order to conserve ballast. But because of the slow ascent, he used up more oxygen. According to his log and the balloon's barograph, he reached 42,470 feet (12,741 m) and then started down. He attempted to vent gas and come down quickly, but he had taken too much time to get so high, and his oxygen

On November 4, 1927, Hawthorne Gray's gondola is prepared for launching from Scott Field near Belleville, Illinois.

ran out. Unwilling to parachute to the ground and lose the record, Gray stubbornly stayed with his balloon. The balloon landed near Sparta, Tennessee, carrying the dead captain. Gray's world record had cost him his life.

Captain Gray's death made it clear that to fly at 40,000 feet (12,000 m) in an open gondola was to invite serious danger. Balloonists in Europe and the United States began to think about how to design an enclosed, pressurized gondola.

The Pressurized Gondola

Auguste Piccard, a Swiss physics professor at the University of Brussels, designed a pressurized gondola in 1930. Piccard was interested in cosmic rays and knew that they could best be studied above the earth's atmosphere, where there was no interference. He chose a balloon rather than a rocket or an airplane to carry his instruments. A balloon could fly higher, stay up longer, and provide a more stable platform.

Piccard's gondola looked like it belonged deep in the sea rather than high in the air. It was an aluminum sphere with two doors and eight small portholes for observation. To supply the gondola with oxygen, Piccard used a device designed for submarines that released pure oxygen into the sealed gondola. At the same time, this device filtered carbon dioxide and other wastes out of the stale cabin air.

In order to keep the gondola at a comfortable temperature during flight,

25

Piccard painted half of it black and left the other half silver. If the balloon's occupants were cold, a propeller would turn the black side toward the sun. Black absorbs the sun's light and, therefore, would heat the gondola. If the temperature rose too high, the silver side, reflecting the sun's light, was turned toward the sun.

With his copilot, Paul Kipfer, Piccard made his first ascent from Augsburg, Germany, on May 27, 1931. The balloon rose quickly and, within 30 minutes, it reached its highest altitude of 51,775 feet (15,533 m). When Piccard and Kipfer tried to descend, however, they discovered the valve line was not working, and they could not vent gas. Finally, as the sun set, the gas began to cool and contract, and the balloon started its descent. The men landed safely in the Bavarian Alps.

The general public and the news media ignored Piccard's scientific discoveries and were only interested in new records. They wanted to know how high each flight went. Soon the Soviet Union and Belgium joined in the race to go higher and higher.

Auguste Piccard's twin brother, Jean, and Jean's wife, Jeannette, were organic chemists living in the United States who became involved in balloon projects. All three were considered somewhat odd for not caring about the altitude records they set. Their only concern was exploring the possibility of flight into the stratosphere.

A balloon designed and built by Jean and Jeannette Piccard, named the *Century of Progress* in honor of Chicago's 100th birthday, was launched on November 20, 1933. Because Chicago did not have the necessary launch facilities, the balloon was sent up from Wright Field outside of Akron, Ohio.

Just before ascending into the stratosphere on May 27, 1931, Auguste Piccard waves to the crowds.

Auguste Piccard came to the U.S. on a lecture tour and was asked to lead a stratosphere flight as part of the celebration of Chicago's 100th anniversary. Business in Europe forced him to withdraw from the project at the beginning, so his brother Jean took over. Here Auguste (left) and Jean examine the *Century of Progress* gondola.

Although it was advertised as a flight designed to break an altitude record, the balloon carried several scientific instruments and experiments. Major Chester Fordney of the United States Marine Corps was responsible for the science experiments, and Tex Settle, a navy lieutenant commander and a balloon racer, was in charge of setting the altitude record.

While Settle used the balloon's radio to talk with the media, Fordney operated a cosmic-ray telescope and experimented with two instruments designed to measure how well certain gases conduct cosmic rays. He also used a *polariscope* to measure the degree of light that is *polarized*, or vibrating in a definite pattern, at high altitudes. For scientists at the University of Illinois, Fordney collected air samples for analysis, and the University of Chicago had stored some single-celled animals and fruit flies in the payload so their researchers could study the effects of high altitude on genetic mutation.

The two men landed at 5:40 P.M. near Bridgeton, New Jersey. Fordney had gathered valuable scientific data, and Settle had set an altitude record of 61,237 feet (18,371 m).

Not satisfied that there had been enough emphasis on scientific investigation, Jeannette and Jean Piccard decided to make a stratospheric trip to study cosmic rays for themselves.

Below: Jeanette and Jean Piccard in the gondola of the *Century of Progress*. Right: The inflated balloon.

Jeannette would pilot the balloon while Jean would conduct the experiments. The National Geographic Society and several government agencies turned down the couple's request for funding. They did not want to be responsible for sending a woman into the stratosphere, especially a woman who was a mother. The Piccards then approached Dr. W.F.G. Swann, one of the foremost cosmic-ray researchers in the United States. He agreed to support their expedition by providing the husband-and-wife team with four Geiger counters to determine the direction of the cosmic rays.

On October 23, 1934, Jeannette Piccard became the first woman to venture into the stratosphere. To the strains of the U.S. national anthem, the *Century*

At 7,000 feet (2,100 m), the torn *Explorer I* resembles a parachute (above). After the gasbag explodes, the fabric and gondola plummet (upper right). A puff of dust in a Nebraska cornfield ends the flight (lower right).

of Progress began its slow ascent. The balloon left the ground at 6:51 A.M. from the airport at Dearborn, Michigan. Jeannette piloted the balloon to 57,579 feet (17,274 m), and Jean turned on the Geiger counters and began his data collection. The team made a safe landing at 2:45 P.M. near Cadiz, Ohio.

At the same time as the Piccards' flights, the National Geographic Society and the U.S. Army Air Corps were conducting their own research with their huge, 307-foot (92-m)-high zero-pressure balloons, *Explorer I* and *Explorer II*. On its first flight, *Explorer I* developed a rip in the gasbag that allowed the rapidly expanding hydrogen, heated by the sun, to mix with air. The air entered the gasbag and became superheated. The balloon exploded, but the three crewmen parachuted to safety.

To prevent future explosions, *Explorer II* was filled with helium. Unlike hydrogen, helium does not explode when heated, but it is twice as heavy. In order to have the same lifting power, the gasbag has to be larger. *Explorer II* was more science oriented than *Explorer I*, and its pressurized gondola would be rotated to make observations. During a flight, scientists would collect upper-air samples and determine the electrical conductivity of the atmosphere at several altitudes. They would gather data on temperature, barometric pressure, wind direction and velocity, and measure the brightness of the sun and the reflection of its rays on the earth. Cosmic-ray studies, fruit-fly experiments, and an investigation of balloon navigation problems were also planned, and photographs would be taken of the activity inside the pressurized gondola and of the view outside the portholes.

Opposite: *Explorer II* during inflation. Above: An inside view of the *Explorer II*'s gondola shows (1) porthole for entrance, (2) porthole for viewing the earth, (3) statoscope to show whether the balloon is rising or falling, (4) cameras to photograph dials of the instruments at short intervals, (5) camera to photograph the horizon, (6) flask to collect air samples, (7) reserve supply of liquid oxygen, (8) hopper to discharge ballast, (9) instrument to record the air's electrical conductivity, (10) compressed oxygen to operate the valves on the top of the balloon, (11) cosmic-ray-counting apparatus, (12) air-conditioning apparatus.

As *Explorer II* is filled with helium, its mooring ropes are slowly let out (right) and the balloon rises from the Stratobowl (above).

Captains Albert W. Stevens and Orvil A. Anderson of the U.S. Army Air Corps lifted off from the Stratobowl, a launch pad outside of Rapid City, South Dakota, in *Explorer II* on November 11, 1935, at 7:01 A.M. By 10:50 A.M., they had reached their record-shattering altitude of 72,395 feet (21,719 m), and they stayed above 70,000 feet (21,000 m) for one hour and 40 minutes. Because the balloon flew so high and the day was cloudless, Stevens and Anderson were the first people to clearly see the curvature of the earth. The balloonists talked by radio to Washington, D.C., San Francisco, California, and London, England, and they were heard in South Africa and Australia. With a mountain of new scientific data and their precious film, Stevens and Anderson landed at 3:14 P.M. on November 11 near White Lake, South Dakota, 230 miles (368 km) from the launch site.

Right: A scientist analyzes air samples taken by *Explorer II*. Below: A photograph of central South Dakota taken from *Explorer II*. Geometrical cultivated fields stand out in sharp contrast to the grasslands and erosional channels carved by rain water that drains into the South Fork of the White River.

New Balloon Materials

In the 1920s and 1930s, latex rubber was commonly used in balloon construction. But because rubber balloons were heavy, Jean Piccard and scientist John Ackerman of the University of Minnesota began to experiment with cellophane balloons. Although cellophane had a tendency to crack in cold temperatures, Piccard and Ackerman performed several successful ground-controlled flights. Launched from the athletic stadium at the University of Minnesota on June 24, 1936, their first balloon stayed aloft 10 hours and traveled 613 miles (981 km).

During World War II, the General Mills company of Minneapolis, Minnesota, manufactured bombsights and other military equipment. The Piccards and their partner, engineer Otto C. Winzen, persuaded General Mills to assist them with a new project—Helios. Helios would consist of 80-100 plastic balloons tied together. The balloons could be cut loose one at a time to make a controlled descent. Still dreaming of piloted flight, Jean and Jeannette Piccard hoped to ride over 100,000 feet (30,000 m) inside of their pressurized gondola. The Office of Naval Research (ONR) offered them funding if Jeannette would be replaced by a navy pilot for the flight.

Since the air would be very cold at 100,000 feet (30,000 m), the Piccards' first task was to find a plastic that was more durable than cellophane. Winzen developed a thin plastic material

One of John Ackerman's cellophane balloons is launched at the University of Minnesota on June 24, 1936.

called *polyethylene*. During several test flights, the balloons reached 100,000 feet (30,000 m). But the gasbags came back full of leaky seams, so they would not be safe enough for human passengers. Helios was dropped by the ONR in favor of Skyhook, a series of single plastic balloons that were ground-controlled and had payloads designed to study cosmic rays.

Disappointed, the Piccards left the project in 1949 to pursue other scientific interests. Otto Winzen and his wife, Vera, left at the same time to start Winzen Research, Inc., of Minneapolis, Minnesota, which later became Winzen International, Inc. Today the company remains a leader in the field of ballooning.

Sending people into the stratosphere was exciting, but it was also very expensive. A gasbag had to be large enough to lift its human cargo and the pressurized gondola that was necessary for human survival, and much time and money had to be spent on safety precautions because human lives were involved. Therefore, scientists who were still interested in exploring the stratosphere turned to the use of unpiloted balloons. Soon lightweight plastic balloons became popular as a low-cost method of putting scientific instruments into the sky.

By 1972, zero-pressure balloons that could carry payloads of 14,000 pounds (6,300 kg) were constructed. These workhorses could fly through winds of 155 mph (248 km/h) and withstand temperatures of -123°F (-86°C) at the edge of the earth's atmosphere. Ninety-six percent of these balloons returned to earth safely, with their instruments intact.

Just prior to launching, a Winzen zero-pressure balloon is swept through the air by the wind.

A launch crew inflates a zero-pressure balloon at the National Scientific Balloon Facility in Palestine, Texas.

4

Investigating the Stratosphere

While pollution drift has been an important area for scientific investigation in the lower atmosphere, the *ozone layer* and drifts of sulfuric acid and radioactive particles are the main areas under investigation in the upper atmosphere.

The Ozone Layer

On September 15, 1982, Jim Anderson could not take his eyes off the 700-foot (210-m)-tall silver balloon shimmering in the Texas heat like a mirage. As it rose into the clear blue morning sky, Anderson, a chemistry professor at Harvard University, thought about the 10 years he had waited for this moment. Anderson had launched 23 other balloon experiments during his career as a scientist. These flights had allowed him only brief glimpses of the stratosphere, and their fixed instruments could only obtain quick samples while the payload, released from the balloon, drifted down through the atmosphere on a parachute. To sample the same layer of the atmosphere more than once during the same flight, this zero-pressure balloon contained a special reel-down device that Anderson and his team had designed.

Anderson's invention consisted of a platform with a radio-controlled winch mounted on it. Similar to a fishing reel, the winch was wound with a 10-mile (16-km)-long piece of strong cord made from Kevlar. A box of scientific instruments hung from the end of the cord. As the balloon descended, Anderson hoped to reel the box of instruments up and down to sample and resample parts of the atmosphere. Dr. Janie Phillips and five other scientists had come from Boston with Anderson to the National Scientific Balloon Facility—the "balloon base," as frequent users call it—outside of Palestine, Texas, to work on the payload and prepare for the launch.

The scientists watched the balloon rise into the upper atmosphere where, at 133,000 feet (39,900 m), it would

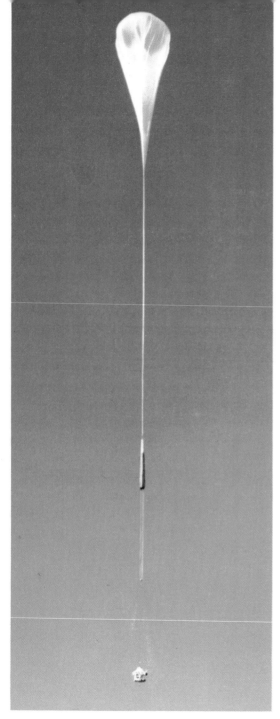

A zero-pressure balloon begins to rise with its payload.

begin to sample the ozone layer. A big problem facing the earth is the gradual destruction of this relatively thin, delicate zone of the stratosphere. Located 10 to 20 miles (16-32 km) above the earth within the stratosphere, the ozone layer absorbs *ultraviolet* radiation from the sun. If this layer were completely destroyed, all of the ultraviolet rays that the sun gives off would reach the earth. These burning rays would decrease crop production, increase skin cancer, and alter the earth's weather and climate.

Three hours and 20 minutes after launch, Anderson's balloon and its precious cargo reached the top of the ozone layer. There the payload, including the reel-down device, was released from the balloon to begin its descent back to earth by parachute. Via radio, Anderson made the winch slowly lower the box of instruments down from the platform. Almost immediately, the instruments began to radio back a stream of data on the amount of atomic oxygen (O) in the upper atmosphere. No one had ever gotten so much information from one flight.

Ozone (O_3) is made up of three parts oxygen. If atomic oxygen attaches itself to ozone, it will break the ozone into oxygen (O_2), thus turning protective ozone into nonprotective oxygen. By measuring the amount of atomic oxygen, Anderson's team could find out how much the ozone layer was being destroyed.

As the instruments hanging from Anderson's balloon descended through the bottom of the ozone layer, they

Viewed through a powerful telescope, a fully-inflated zero-pressure balloon at 120,000 feet (36,000 m) above the earth has expanded to more than 400 feet (120 m) in diameter.

were simply reeled back up to continue measuring until the platform itself reached low altitude. The box of instruments was recovered about 25 miles (40 km) from the balloon base.

With the invention of the reel-down device, Anderson and the many other scientists who study the upper atmosphere could get much more data from each flight. They could discover whether the ozone layer is being broken down by nitrogen compounds and by manufactured chemicals called *fluorocarbons*. Nitrogen compounds occur naturally, and fluorocarbons were used as propellants in cans of spray deodorant, hair spray, and whipped cream in the 1970s.

After the data was collected from the instruments that hung from Anderson's reel-down device, it was assembled on a graph. The graph would be used to develop computer models of what was happening—and what probably will happen—in the upper atmosphere.

Cloud Cover

Balloons have also been used to photograph cloud cover. Using four huge zero-pressure balloons, Robert Watson, coordinator for the Stratospheric Balloon Intercomparison Campaign (SBIC), and other scientists sent gondolas to a height of 125,000 feet (37,500 m) in the autumn of 1982 and the spring of 1983.

By mounting a camera on each balloon and pointing it downward, they were able to photograph the top of the cloud cover. These pictures helped to determine the amount of solar radiation reflected back to the balloon from the clouds. This gave scientists a measurement of how much radiation is reflected by clouds into space and how well the earth is being protected by cloud cover.

The launch and recovery of three of the SBIC's balloon experiments went smoothly, but the gondola on the fourth balloon accidently detached itself. Its parachute failed to open, and the payload fell 108,000 feet (32,400 m) to earth. Only one disc of film survived, and several million dollars worth of instruments were destroyed.

Sulfuric Acid Drift

Volcanic activity has increased in recent years, and so the sulfur dioxide that volcanos spew into the upper atmosphere has also increased. When combined with water and atomic oxygen, sulfur dioxide forms droplets of sulfuric acid, which remain suspended in the atmosphere. The cool air at high altitudes causes the droplets to form clouds, and these clouds can cause

temperatures on the earth's surface to decrease about $2°F$ $(1°C)$ because they partially block sunlight. Knowing the size and density of the clouds allows scientists to predict changes in the world's climate.

Some volcanic eruptions, such as the eruption of Mexico's El Chichon in April 1982, have resulted in long-lasting concentrations of sulfuric acid in the upper atmosphere. Others have barely affected the upper atmosphere. In the state of Washington in 1980, Mount St. Helens spewed its ashes higher than any volcano since 1971. The particles emitted were large and heavy, however, so they fell back to earth quite rapidly.

Using balloons also allows researchers to track the drift of sulfuric acid. The fallout from El Chichon stayed near the equator for about nine months. Nearly a year later, the cloud was over Antarctica.

Technological Problems

High-altitude balloons can also be used to check on the impact of technological problems. On January 24, 1978, a Russian satellite, *Cosmos-954*, reentered the atmosphere over northern Canada. Scientists were concerned that radioactive debris from the satellite's on-board reactor might contaminate the earth's atmosphere.

The U.S. Department of Energy sent up several balloons to check on this possible danger. Rising to an altitude of 24 miles (39 km), these balloons

Mount St. Helens erupts on May 18, 1980, spewing sulfur dioxide into the atmosphere.

carried special filter papers that could detect the presence of radioactive uranium isotopes. When papers were tested for radioactivity, droplets containing uranium were found only at the top of the stratosphere above the polar regions of the earth, so there was no threat to human beings.

Auguste Piccard prepares for launch in an enclosed gondola. This gondola is similar to the one that he and Audouin Dollfus designed for viewing Mars and Venus.

Studying
the Cosmos

An answer to one question almost always raises several more. Once the makeup of the earth's atmosphere was analyzed by low-altitude and stratospheric balloons, scientists wanted to know how the earth's atmosphere differed from the atmosphere of other planets.

Balloon-Borne Telescopes

The first balloon-borne telescope was designed and launched at the Meudon Observatory in Meudon, France, on May 30, 1954, to discover the amount of water vapor in the atmosphere of Mars. A balloon-borne telescope was used because astronomers wanted to be beyond most of the earth's water vapor in the lower atmosphere to view Mars.

The zero-pressure balloon rose to an altitude of 21,000 feet (6,300 m). Using a reflecting telescope with a filter that isolated the water vapor, astronomers Charles Dollfus and his son, Audouin,

observed the Martian atmosphere. They found no evidence of water, so they concluded that there could be no life on Mars.

In 1959, Audouin Dollfus, Auguste Piccard, and several of their colleagues designed and launched a payload for further study of the atmospheres of Mars and Venus. They used a larger telescope, which was mounted in a sealed, spherical gondola designed by Piccard.

To lift the gondola, the team used 104 expandable neoprene rubber balloons in groups of three, spaced 40 feet (12 m) apart on a nylon rope. As the first balloons rose above the intended cruise altitude, they burst, keeping the gondola carrying the astronomer from going any higher. When the observations were completed, a radio control released several more balloons, causing the payload to descend. This flight, and several other observations from a balloon and from a telescope on a mountain top, showed that there

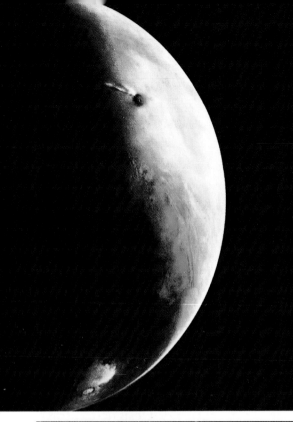

is only a trace of water vapor in the atmosphere of Venus and very little in the Martian atmosphere—probably neither atmosphere has enough water to sustain life.

Today, several improvements have been made in balloons used for astronomical observation. *Infrared*, or heat-sensitive, telescopes are more powerful, and telescopes are fitted with a gyroscope, which keeps the telescope fixed relative to the stars, even when a balloon is revolving in the windy upper atmosphere.

Left: A view of Mars showing a volcano at the top, a crater near the middle, and a crater basin at the bottom. Below: A spiral galaxy.

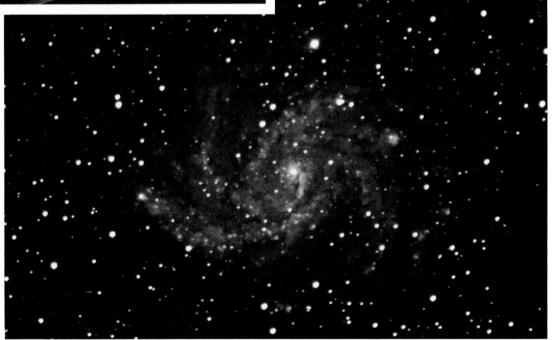

In 1988, a balloon with gamma-ray detectors was launched to observe Supernova 1987A, the first star since 1604 to explode so close to the earth. The detectors showed that Supernova 1987A is moving away from the earth more than four times faster than other nearby stars. Astronomers want future balloon payloads to include instruments that detect X rays, or high-energy particles. Heavenly bodies that emit X rays include *neutron stars*, collapsed stars with billions of densely packed neutrons; *black holes*, collapsed stars so condensed that light and matter cannot escape their gravity; and *white dwarfs*, stars that are nearer the size of the earth but weigh as much as the sun.

Vega 1 and *Vega 2*

After decades of working independently, Soviet-bloc and Western nations joined together to establish the Interagency Consultative Group (IACG) to coordinate joint space activity. Their first project was to make a detailed exploration of Venus with two balloons. French scientist Jacques E. Blamont had first proposed the idea in 1967, but the experiments were not launched until 1984.

The U.S.S.R. launched the *Vega 1* and *Vega 2* spacecraft on December 15 and December 21, 1984, respectively. They made the 64-million-mile (102-million-km) journey to Venus in six months. *Vega 1* reached Venus on June 10 and *Vega 2* on June 15, 1985. As each spacecraft flew by the planet, it

deployed a capsule that would enter the Venusian atmosphere. The spacecraft then fired their engines to move away from a collision with Venus and toward a meeting with Comet Halley.

Each capsule entered Venus' atmosphere at 78 miles (125 km) above the planet. At 40 miles (64 km), a parachute opened to slow the capsule's descent. As it descended, the capsule released two items—a balloon with its payload and a lander with scientific instruments. Each lander rode the parachute to the planet's surface. There, its instruments recorded a temperature of 860°F (460°C) and showed the surface air pressure to be 100 times greater than that of the earth's at sea level.

The balloons that were released inflated automatically. Designed to travel for 46 hours around Venus, they carried payloads weighing only 14 pounds (6 kg). Inside each of the small gondolas was a battery, electronic instruments to collect and transmit data, and an antenna. The balloon data would be received by 20 tracking stations, located on every continent except Antarctica. Transmission time from Venus to earth was six minutes. Scientific instruments on board included sensors to measure temperature and air pressure, a bladelike device that measured wind velocity, a photometer to measure lightning flashes, and a detector for measuring the abundance of cloud particles.

At an altitude of 34 miles (54 km), instrument readings showed that air

After dropping off a small weather balloon to measure Venus' atmosphere and a landing module to test the planet's surface, the *Vega* spacecraft will travel on its way to Comet Halley.

pressure was 60 times that of the earth's air pressure at sea level. Even that far from the surface, air temperature was 100°F (38°C). Venus is a much hotter planet than earth because it is much closer to the sun and because the sun also shines longer on the surface of Venus. Yet the surface is also dark longer, because the planet rotates very slowly. The sun only rises every 117 earth days.

Both balloons had entered Venus' atmosphere in the dark, and they were expected to burst as soon as they reached hot sunlight—but they didn't. Each balloon's battery continued operating for several hours in the sunlight, and the batteries actually ran down before the balloons burst.

The balloons traveled at 150 mph (240 km/h) in an east-to-west direction at Venus' equator. They covered

7,200 miles (11,520 km) of Venus' surface, or one-third of its circumference.

Plans are underway to explore Mars using an observation platform carried by two balloons: a closed, helium-filled balloon to keep the platform aloft at night and an open balloon to raise the payload during the day.

Astronomical Balloons

Many astronomical balloons are launched from the National Scientific Balloon Facility near Palestine, Texas. Most launches take place in the spring or autumn when stratospheric winds are calm.

Early on a clear, windless day, a large payload is being prepared for launch. The launch vehicle, nicknamed Tiny Tim, carries the payload, which is attached to the balloon and parachute by steel cables.

Two balloons are being inflated. While Tiny Tim (foreground) holds the payload, a tie-down vehicle (background) keeps the closer balloon from straining at the payload until it is fully inflated.

At about 1:00 P.M, Tiny Tim, the huge, 52-ton (47-tonne) launch vehicle, rolls over to the balloon base at 5 mph (8 km/h) on wheels 8 feet (240 cm) tall to pick up the payload. When Tiny Tim arrives at the launchpad, the balloon is brought out. The fragile plastic zero-pressure balloon, about as thick as a dry cleaner's bag, and the gondola's parachute are carefully unfolded and checked for holes. Even the tiniest hole would start a rip that could shred the whole balloon when it is fully inflated.

A helium truck pulls up. Workers attach hoses to the balloon, and a noisy inflation begins. Slowly, a shimmering bubble forms at the top of the balloon. A tie-down vehicle with a large spool turned sideways holds the bottom of the balloon to keep it from straining at the payload and damaging itself.

Launched from the National Scientific Balloon Facility near Palestine, Texas, on June 12, 1986, a partially filled zero-pressure balloon is held to the ground by the tie-down vehicle.

Carrying payloads for research in high-energy astrophysics, astronomy, and the upper atmosphere, a zero-pressure balloon ascends from the launch site.

After 45 minutes, the huge transparent balloon is fully inflated.

Now, the spool on the tie-down vehicle turns to release the balloon, still held by a Kevlar line attached to the payload. The balloon rises until the line between gasbag and payload is taut. When the balloon is directly overhead, Tiny Tim releases the payload, and balloon and cargo quickly disappear into the sky.

Within two hours, the balloon reaches its float altitude of 95,000 feet (28,500 m). Pilots in a chase plane follow at a lower altitude, communicating with the balloon through a radio decoder. The decoder activates motors, changes the direction of the telescope, and releases the payload at the end of the flight.

With the balloon at float altitude, the radio commands the telescope to begin observing the first cosmic target. The telescope "sees" with chips of a detector material that becomes warm when hit by infrared radiation. All objects give off infrared rays in relation to their temperature. In the telescope, infrared rays from stars and planets warm the detector material. This warmth produces a change in voltage in the telescope, which tells the astronomers how bright the object is. The detector material is placed in liquid helium to keep it very cool so its own heat will not confuse the readings. It is so sensitive that astronomers can "see" stars anywhere in the Milky Way galaxy, no matter how hidden they are by dust.

When 15 to 20 cosmic targets have been examined, the payload is released from the balloon by radio command. The delicate instruments float back to earth via the on-board parachute. A crew from the balloon base goes out to retrieve the instruments. If they are lucky, the payload will land in an open field, instead of in a swamp or tree.

Although most balloons are launched from the balloon base near Palestine, Texas, the facility at the University of Wyoming at Laramie is used for launching expandable balloons that are used in researching sulfuric acid drift. These smaller balloons are easier to send up than the huge zero-pressure balloons and can be launched just a few hours after a volcano erupts. The Laramie Small Scientific Balloon Program has launched balloons from such diverse places as Panama, Australia, Alaska, and Antarctica.

In special situations, a new launching base may be built. An example is the base at Watukosek, East Java, Indonesia. In 1983, there was a solar eclipse that could be viewed from Indonesia, a group of islands in the South Pacific. Astronomers from Japan and Indonesia wanted to study the *F corona*, the light around the sun that is scattered by interplanetary dust. The F corona is quite faint and can be seen clearly only at the time of a solar eclipse. The astronomers wanted to use a balloon to get a telescope above the earth's atmosphere, which would absorb the infrared rays they wished to observe.

On June 11, 1983, the team launched a balloon from their newly constructed balloon base at Watukosek. The payload included the infrared telescope and a Silicon Intensifier Target (SIT) television camera to photograph the F corona. Both camera and telescope were kept pointed at the eclipse by radio control.

When the balloon reached its cruise altitude, it began flying west-southwest. The telescope and the camera each picked up extra brightness around the western edge of the sun. Astronomers think that this may be due to a hot dust cloud near one side of the F corona.

A scientific payload is recovered from a swamp after a flight.

51

A Telescope for Space

Many people interested in exploring the heavens dream of a large, powerful telescope that can be either flown aboard a space shuttle or installed on a permanent space station. A space telescope has to be lightweight, since all launch vehicles have limited cargo capacity, and stable so that it will be easy to keep focused once it is set up.

In 1983, the National Aeronautics and Space Administration (NASA) hired three astronomers to design a space telescope, which was to be test-flown in a balloon. Balloon flights can be made more frequently and are less expensive than satellite launches, and balloons can also be put into lower orbits than satellites.

Astronomers wanted the new telescope to measure at least 10 feet (3 m)

Mounted on the Space Shuttle for launch into orbit, NASA's Space Telescope—the most powerful telescope ever built—enables scientists to gaze seven times farther into space than before.

After the Space Shuttle has launched the Space Telescope, astronomers should be able to look at quasars, galaxies, gaseous nebulae, and stars that are 50 times fainter than those seen by the most powerful telescopes on the ground.

in diameter. To stabilize such a large instrument, a motorized mechanism, activated by a gyroscope, was designed. The gyroscope will "tell" the mechanism when the telescope is becoming unstable, which will then turn on the motor to move the telescope into a more stable position.

The greatest challenge was to develop a mirror for the 1,889-pound (850-kg) telescope. It had to be as lightweight as possible and withstand hot summer ground temperatures and changes to the colder temperatures of −40°F to −58°F (−40°C to −50°C) at the edge of the earth's atmosphere. It also had to survive a parachute landing! After extensive testing, the astronomers decided to use carbon-fiber reinforced plastic with a honeycomb aluminum core. NASA is also considering funding for an 80-inch (200-centimeter) telescope that would give astronomers an even closer look at the stars.

Astronauts Malcolm Ross (left) and M. Lee Lewis, and flight surgeon Captain Norman Lee Barr watch as a project engineer (right) is handed instruments from *Strato-Lab I's* open hatch.

Simulating
Space Travel

Although early scientists went up with their balloons, it soon became clear the research could be done with ground-controlled balloons. For cost and safety reasons, most scientists, therefore, stayed on the ground while their balloons explored the atmosphere.

In the late 1950s, however, the military began to reconsider piloted balloon flights. Military pilots needed to learn about the problems they might face when flying above 100,000 feet (30,000 m), and there was talk of a piloted space program starting as soon as rockets could be reliably launched. The military wanted to test high-altitude equipment, such as parachutes, pressure garments, and life-support systems, and they also wanted to learn more about aerospace medicine.

Both the navy and the air force established a program of piloted balloon training flights. The navy's program was called Strato-Lab. Piloted by naval officers Malcolm Ross and M. Lee Lewis, the *Strato-Lab I* flight rose to a record altitude of 76,000 feet (22,800 m) on November 8, 1956. Despite a valve failure that caused a very rapid descent, the giant balloon was finally slowed down enough to land safely.

At the same time, the air force began its own series of high-altitude balloon flights, Manhigh. The Manhigh capsule was a cylinder closer in size to the small, cone-shaped Mercury capsule used by the original seven astronauts than the balloon gondolas the Piccards had invented. It looked like a cross between a large scuba tank and the periscope on a submarine and was just big enough to hold one person. The pilot wore a partial-pressure suit and sat in a nylon mesh seat, surrounded by life-support devices and scientific instruments.

The polyethylene balloon was made by Winzen Research, Inc. The capsule and its parachute could be released from the balloon to float back to earth either by a command from the pilot or the ground control. It could be pro-

Below: A launch crew inflates *Strato-Lab I*'s gasbag. **Right:** Lewis and Ross prepare to take off inside *Strato-Lab I*'s pressurized gondola.

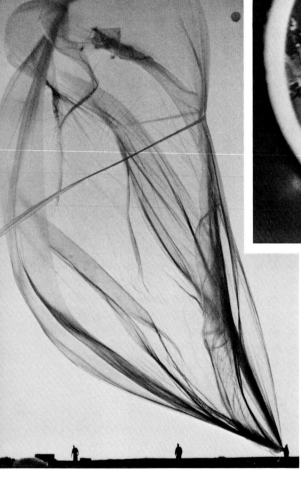

grammed to release the balloon at sunset on the second day of flight.

The first Manhigh pilot was Captain Joe Kittinger, a U.S. Air Force test pilot who later became the first person to make a solo flight in a balloon across the Atlantic Ocean. *Manhigh I*, a huge zero-pressure balloon with a pressurized gondola, began its ascent on June 2, 1957, at 6:23 A.M. from Fleming field in South Saint Paul, Minnesota. Within two hours, Kittinger had reached a dizzying altitude of 96,000 feet (28,800 m). Then his voice communication system failed, and he had to establish communication with the base, called a *downlink*, via a Morse code transmitter. When Kittinger suddenly signaled that his oxygen bottle was only half-full, he was ordered to begin an immediate descent. He had enough bottled air to reach the oxygen-rich part of the atmosphere where breathing was no problem, but he landed at 12:57 P.M. with an empty oxygen bottle.

A check of the oxygen system revealed that a connection had been installed backward, so oxygen had been pumped out of the gondola. A faulty switch had caused the voice communication system to fail. When these systems had been repaired, it was time for *Manhigh II*. This time, the pilot would be Major David G. Simons, a physician and head of the Space Biology Branch at Holloman Air Force Base in New Mexico.

Manhigh II was sent aloft near Crosby, Minnesota, at 9:22 A.M. on August 19, 1957. To protect the tall balloon from wind damage, it was launched from a deep pit. This pre-Sputnik craft reached an altitude of 102,000 feet (30,600 m) and stayed there all day. Simons spent his time observing space with a telescope, taking pictures, and measuring sky brightness with a spot photometer.

As the sky darkened at sunset, the balloon's helium cooled, and the craft descended to 84,000 feet (25,200 m). By dropping two large batteries, Simons was able to stay above 70,000 feet (21,000 m) and avoid a thunderstorm beneath him. At sunrise, he could still see lightning below, so he let the expanding helium take the balloon to 90,000 feet (27,000 m). Later in the day, 32 hours and 10 minutes after takeoff, he finally was able to land. Because Simons showed no adverse effects from being in space for almost a day and a half, air force officials quickly approved a third Manhigh flight.

The air force selected *Manhigh III*'s pilot carefully, much the same way that future space explorers would be chosen.

Six candidates submitted their resumes and went through a four-day medical examination. All six men were given extensive psychiatric examinations, were immersed in ice water, spent an hour in a "hot box" (155°F (68°C) and 85 percent humidity), had a session in the centrifuge, and were confined to the Manhigh capsule for 24 hours, as they would be on an actual flight.

The man finally chosen to pilot *Manhigh III* was 25-year-old air force engineer Lt. Clifton McClure. Because of cold weather in Minnesota, *Manhigh III* was launched from Holloman Air Force Base in New Mexico on October 6, 1958.

Shortly after lift-off, McClure accidently opened the parachute he was wearing. He knew the air force personnel would make him return if he mentioned it, so with barely enough room to turn around, he repacked the yards of silk. His heavy perspiration overloaded the moisture-removing capacity of his life-support system, however, and the extra moisture reacted with the carbon dioxide-removing chemical to produce heat. McClure became exhausted, and his temperature rose to 101°F (38°C). He was ordered to return to the ground, but that took more than five hours because the balloon was at 99,700 feet (29,910 m). By the time he landed, McClure's temperature was 108°F (42°C), but he was still able to walk from the capsule to a waiting helicopter. McClure's flight marked the end of the Manhigh project and the beginning of rocket-powered spaceflight.

Before sending *Echo II* aloft early in 1964, small 30-foot (9-m) helium-filled balloons carry engineers aloft to check the satellite's ability to reflect radio frequencies.

7

Bringing Us Closer

In the days before air travel, the only way to communicate with the world outside of one's own continent was by letter, which took several weeks, or by a personal visit, which involved a long sea journey. Today, people around the world visit with each other, do business, and are entertained with the help of communications satellites. The original satellites were really balloons.

One of the early satellites was a super-pressure balloon that stayed in orbit for eight years. *Echo I* was launched in the nose of a Delta rocket on August 12, 1960. At a predetermined altitude, an explosive charge split open the balloon's container, and the balloon quickly inflated. As the sun warmed the air, chemicals inside the balloon vaporized to further inflate the balloon.

Echo I relayed almost instantaneous communications from the United States to Europe. Two solar-powered radio beacons on board the balloon helped scientists and engineers track and locate it. Then sound waves were sent to the balloon at an angle so they would bounce off its surface at the same angle to the other continent. U.S. President Dwight Eisenhower announced that any nation was welcome to use *Echo I* for its own experiments.

Circling the earth every two hours, *Echo I* traveled more than one billion miles (1.6 billion km). Bombarded by micrometeorites and space dust, it finally began to leak, and then collapsed. It fell back into the atmosphere, burning up on June 23, 1968.

In 1964, *Echo II* was launched. The success of the Echo series paved the way for the next generation of balloon satellites. These balloons inflated when rockets propelled them into orbit, and their filmy skins disintegrated when they were exposed to the sunlight, leaving a rigid wire-mesh ball in orbit. The mesh was an excellent reflector of radio waves.

Another generation of inflatable satellites was the Explorer series. Made of plastic and aluminum foil, *Explorer IX* was launched on February 16, 1961. It studied air density, solar radiation, and air pressure, and stayed in orbit for several years.

Through the use of these balloons, scientists and engineers learned that by bouncing sound waves off an object at a high altitude, they are able to communicate with people all over the world. By the time the last Explorer balloon satellite stopped functioning, noninflatable satellites, which had longer lives and refueling capabilities, were well on their way to regular use.

Left: NASA technicians conduct inflation tests on *Echo II* before it joins *Echo I* in space orbit. Above: *Explorer IX* is launched on February 16, 1961.

The Future of the Balloon

The future of scientific balloons looks promising. Balloons can be folded into a small space and easily lifted into orbit and then rapidly inflated, or they can be sent up from a balloon launch facility. They can be made of plastic and fiber that are as strong as steel but much lighter, or they can be made of light, fragile plastic. And balloons have many uses.

Scientists are currently using balloon-borne telescopes to record showers of cosmic rays and to observe a recent supernova. They want to identify the particles and energies that make up the *atomic nucleus*, the center of the atom that contains protons and neutrons.

Scientists will continue to use balloons to learn more and more about heavenly bodies, pollution drift, the ozone layer, and the effectiveness of anything that may one day be launched in space. In a November 1983 interview for *Sky and Telescope*, Alfred Shipley, director of the balloon base at Palestine, Texas, said, "I do not believe the balloon will fade into obscurity for a long time to come. And even if it does, it will likely be rediscovered once more by future generations."

At sunset, a research balloon is inflated for a nighttime astronomy experiment.

GLOSSARY

atomic nucleus: the large, center part of the atom containing protons and neutrons

barograph: an instrument that measures variations of air pressure in relation to altitude

cosmic rays: high-energy particles that penetrate the earth's upper atmosphere and produce non-harmful radiation

expandable balloon: a balloon with a sealed gasbag containing gas that expands as the balloon rises. The expanding gas bursts the balloon and the payload returns to earth by parachute.

free radicals: atoms having at least one unpaired electron. (Atomic oxygen (O) is an example.)

gasbag: the large, round part of the balloon—sometimes called the envelope—that holds gases such as hydrogen, helium, or warm air

hygrometer: an instrument used in the 18th and early 19th centuries to measure the amount of water vapor in the air by means of changes in the length of human hair. Wound around a spool, the piece of hair shortened as it became drier and stretched as it became moist.

infrared: a type of radiation with wavelengths longer than those of visible light but shorter than microwaves. Its presence is an indicator of heat.

meteorological balloon: an expandable balloon used to measure pressure, temperature, humidity, and wind velocity in the upper atmosphere

ozone layer: a region of the stratosphere containing a high amount of ozone (O_3) that absorbs ultraviolet rays from the sun

payload: the scientific instruments carried by a balloon

polarized: light waves that vibrate on only one plane in a definite pattern

radiosonde: a small, portable weather station—attached to a balloon and linked by radio to the ground—that measures temperature, humidity, and air pressure

stratosphere: the atmosphere from 7 miles (11 km) to 30 miles (50 km) above the earth.

superpressure balloon: a balloon with a sealed gasbag that is inflated so the inside air pressure is slightly higher than the outside air pressure. This causes the balloon to rise to a predetermined altitude and float at a constant level of air pressure

thermal inversion: a condition in which air near the ground is cool and moist while the air above it is warmer and drier. The air near the ground is trapped under the warmer air and, therefore, cannot rise.

valve: to pull a cord that opens a valve in the top of the gasbag, causing the balloon to descend

zero-pressure balloon: a balloon with an opening from which gas can escape when it has expanded to fill the gasbag. The pressure inside the balloon stays the same as the outside air.

INDEX

ACKNOWLEDGMENTS: The photographs in this book are reproduced through the courtesy of: pp. 1, 28, Dearborn Historical Museum; pp. 2, 30, 31, 32 (bottom), Richard H. Stewart, © 1936 National Geographic Society; p. 6, Library of Congress; pp. 8, 10, 11, 15, 22, 25, 27, Smithsonian Institution; pp. 9, 14, 18, 19, National Center for Atmospheric Research; p. 12, Harvard University; p. 17, National Oceanic and Atmospheric Association; p. 21, Sandia National Laboratories; pp. 26, 42, The Bettmann Archive; p. 29, M/Sgt. Gilbert, © 1934 National Geographic Society; p. 32 (top), Sgt. G.B. Gilbert and Capt. H.K. Baisley, © 1936 National Geographic Society; p. 33 (top), Edwin L. Wisherd, © 1936 National Geographic Society; p. 33 (bottom), Capt. A.W. Stevens, © 1936 National Geographic Society; p. 34, University of Minnesota Archives; pp. 35, 36, 39, 47, 48, 50, 51, 61, Winzen International, Inc.; pp. 38, 44, 49, 52, 53, 58, 60, NASA; p. 41, U.S. Geological Survey; p. 46, Novosti; pp. 54, 56 (right), Thomas J. Abercrombie, © 1957 National Geographic Society; p. 56 (left), Lynn Abercrombie, © 1957 National Geographic Society. Cover photographs courtesy of Winzen International (front) and Richard H. Stewart, © 1936 National Geographic Society (back).